David and Goliath

First published in 1999 by Franklin Watts
96 Leonard Street, London EC2A 4XD

Franklin Watts Australia
14 Mars Road
Lane Cove
NSW 2066

Text copyright © Franklin Watts 1999
Illustrations copyright © Diana Mayo 1999

Series editor: Rachel Cooke
Art director: Robert Walster and Jonathan Hair
Consultants: Reverend Richard Adfield;
Marlena Schmool and Samantha Blendis,
Board of Deputies of British Jews

A CIP catalogue record for this book
is available from the British Library.

ISBN 0 7496 3217 8

Dewey Classification 221

Printed in Hong Kong/China

David and Goliath

Retold by Mary Auld

Illustrated by Diana Mayo

W

FRANKLIN WATTS

NEW YORK•LONDON•SYDNEY

Long ago, the people of Israel asked the prophet Samuel to choose them a king. Samuel prayed and spoke to God and, at God's wish, he chose a man called Saul to be the Israelites' king.

Saul was a brave warrior, but he did not always listen to God or follow His commands. God became unhappy with Saul as king, and He spoke again to the prophet Samuel.

"You must visit the town of Bethlehem," He told Samuel. "Take a heifer with you as a sacrifice and go to the house of Jesse. Ask Jesse and his family to help you with the sacrifice. Then I shall point out one of his sons, whom you must anoint with oil. This son shall one day be king of Israel."

And Samuel set out for Bethlehem.

When he arrived, Samuel went
straight to Jesse's house. He told Jesse
and his family to prepare for the
sacrifice and a feast. As the family
gathered together, Samuel met Jesse's
eldest son, Eliab. Surely, Samuel
thought, this handsome man would
be God's choice. But God said to him,

"Don't judge Eliab by his appearance.
He is not my choice. Remember, you
can only see what a man looks like.
I can see into his heart." So Samuel
passed on to Jesse's next son, and the
one after that, and then yet another,
until he had seen seven of his sons.
But still God did not show His choice.

"Haven't you any other sons?"
Samuel asked Jesse.

"There is only my youngest, David,
who is away looking after the sheep,"
replied Jesse.

So David was sent for and brought
before Samuel. The boy was rosy-cheeked
and bright-eyed. "This is the one," said
God to Samuel. Then the prophet arose
and anointed David with oil. From that
day onwards, the spirit of God filled
David and was always with him.

Meanwhile, King Saul was ill. God had set an evil spirit on him, which teased and terrified him. "We must find someone who can play the harp," said Saul's courtiers. "The music will soothe the king."

Saul ordered his attendants to find a good harp-player, and one of them thought of the shepherd David. A message went to Jesse asking for his son, so Jesse sent David to the king, together with a donkey laden with gifts: bread, wine and a young goat.

Saul liked David very much. Whenever the evil spirit came upon the king, David would pick up his harp and play, and Saul would relax and the evil spirit leave him.

Sometime after, the Philistines gathered an army together to fight against Israel. Saul and the Israelites prepared for battle, too.

The Israelites pitched their camp on
one hill and the Philistines on another,
with the narrow valley of Elah
between them.

A champion came forward from the Philistine ranks called Goliath of Gath. He was a giant of a man, standing over nine feet tall. His helmet and body armour were all made of gleaming bronze, as was the javelin slung across his back. The point of his massive spear was made of iron. His shield-bearer marched in front of him.

Goliath shouted across to the Israelite army. "Why do you need to fight a battle? Instead, choose one man to fight me - if he kills me, the Philistines will become your slaves, but if I kill him, you will become our slaves and serve us."

Goliath's challenge terrified Saul and all his people. Who could possibly take on such a man?

At this time, David had returned to his father Jesse to tend the sheep, but his three eldest brothers served in Saul's army. Jesse said to David, "Take this food to your brothers in the valley of Elah and bring me back news of them."

Early next morning, David set out as Jesse ordered, leaving someone else in charge of his sheep. He arrived at the Israelite camp just as the soldiers were taking up their battle positions, shouting a war cry. David ran to the battle lines and greeted his people.

Just as David spoke, Goliath stepped
out from the Philistines' ranks and
shouted his challenge once again.
David heard it and saw how the
Israelites fled from the giant in terror.

Word went around the Israelite camp,
"The king will reward whoever kills
Goliath with great wealth - and give
him his daughter in marriage."

David heard the soldiers' talk and
spoke to them. "Who does this
Philistine think he is? How dare he
defy the armies of God?" he asked.

When Eliab, David's eldest brother,

heard this fighting talk, he was furious.
"Why did you come here?" he
demanded. "I know what a show-off
you can be. You are only here to
watch the battle!"

"Now what have I done?" said
David. "I was only asking." And he
turned away and spoke to someone
else about Goliath and the reward.

Soon Saul heard about David's questions and sent for him.

David said to Saul, "Don't be frightened of Goliath. I shall fight him."

"You can't fight the Philistine," replied Saul. "You are just a boy and he has been a warrior for many years."

"I have killed both a lion and a bear to protect my father's sheep," said David. "The Philistine is just like them. God protected me from the claws of the lion and the bear, and He will keep me safe from Goliath."

"Then go," said Saul, "and may God be with you."

Then Saul dressed David in his own tunic. He put a bronze helmet on David's head and a breastplate around his body. David fastened on a sword and then tried walking around.

"I can't wear all this," he said. "I'm just not used to it." So he took off the armour.

Instead, David chose five smooth stones from a nearby stream and put them in his shepherd's bag. He took his staff in one hand and his sling in the other and went to meet Goliath.

23

Goliath and his shield-bearer came forward to meet David. When the Philistine saw that David was just a fresh-faced boy, he laughed nastily and cursed him. "Am I a dog that you mean to fight with a stick? Come here, I'll kill you and feed your body to the birds and animals!" jeered Goliath.

But David was not frightened. He cried out, "You may have your weapons, but I come against you in the name of God. Today, when I strike you down, the whole world will see that there is a God in Israel," and he ran towards Goliath.

Reaching into his bag and taking out a stone, he slung it and struck the Philistine straight on the forehead. The stone sunk in and Goliath toppled forward on to the ground.

David stood over Goliath and cut off his head with the giant's own sword. When the Philistines saw that their champion was dead, they turned and ran. With a war cry, the men of Israel followed them and chased them right to the gates of Ekron, a great Philistine city, killing many as they went.

David took Goliath's head to Jerusalem and brought it before Saul. "Who are you?" Saul asked him in amazement.

"I am the son of your servant Jesse of Bethlehem," said David simply. Perhaps then Saul realised he was looking in the face of the next king of Israel.

About this story

David and Goliath is a retelling of part of I Samuel, one of the books that make up the Bible. The Bible is the name given to the collection of writings that are sacred, in different forms, to the Jewish and Christian religions. I Samuel is one of the 39 books in the Hebrew Bible, Tanakh, or Christian Old Testament.

Who was David?

David was the eighth and youngest son of Jesse of Bethlehem. *David and Goliath* tells how he came to know Saul, the first king of Israel. From these early meetings, David became a member of Saul's court and a close friend of his son Jonathan. Saul began to feel threatened by David's popularity and tried to kill him, forcing him to flee the court. When Saul died in another battle with the Philistines, he left most of Israel under Philistine control, but David managed to become king of Judah (a region of Israel).

From Judah, David reconquered the rest of Israel and became its king, as God had said to Samuel. David later brought all of Canaan under Israelite control and made Jerusalem its capital. With David as its king, Israel became the most powerful country between the rivers Nile and Euphrates. David died around 962 BC after ruling for about 33 years.

Israelites and Philistines

The Israelites were God's chosen people. He had promised them a land of plenty when He freed them from slavery in Egypt. Led by Moses, the Israelites had come to Canaan, 'the promised land', about 250 years before David was born. The Philistines arrived in the region by sea shortly after this and settled along the coast. In the centuries that followed there were constant battles between the two peoples for control of Canaan. Saul became the first king of Israel because of his successes against the Philistines, but it was David who finally defeated them completely.

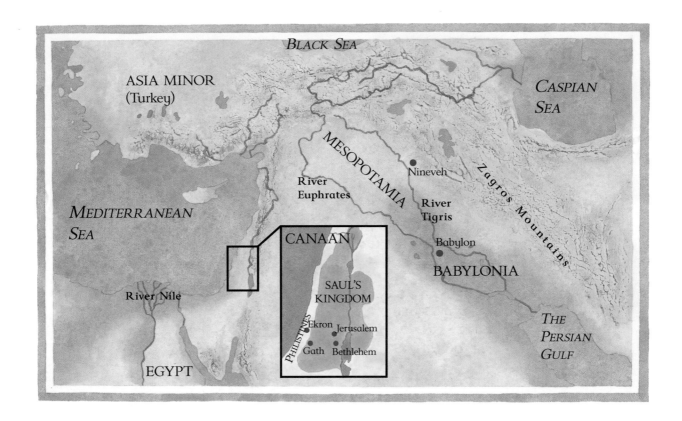

Musician and warrior

David is a great hero of the Bible, but there are two sides to his character - the gifted musician and the ruthless warrior. As a musician and poet, he is traditionally thought to have written many of the Psalms (the collection of poems praising God in the Bible), including Psalm 23, 'The Lord is My Shepherd'. As a soldier and king, he subdued the Philistines but frequently acted unfairly and with cruelty to maintain his power. However, even though he was not a perfect king, he was true to his religion and faithful to God throughout his life. He was viewed by the Israelites as God's chosen ruler, and later prophets said that a Messiah (one chosen by God to save His people) would come from David's family. Christians, who believe Jesus is the Messiah, saw this prophecy fulfilled since Joseph, Jesus's earthly father, was a descendant of David.

Useful words

Anoint To anoint someone, you smear a small amount of oil (or a similar substance) on him or her. In religious ceremonies, anointing someone is a way of showing that he or she is blessed and chosen by God.

Challenge A challenge given in a war is a formal offer of a fight, usually one person against another, to settle the argument.

Champion In a battle, a champion is a person who fights on his own, but usually on behalf of someone else. Goliath fights on his own and on behalf of the whole Philistine army.

Evil Evil is something very bad and wicked, which causes harm to people. In the past, people believed illness was caused by evil, so the 'evil spirit' that troubled Saul may have been some kind of illness.

Heifer A heifer is a young cow that has not yet had a calf.

Israelites Also known as Hebrews, the Israelites were an ancient people from the Middle East amongst whom the Jewish religion began. They took their name from their ancestor Jacob, whom God called Israel, which means 'to struggle to understand God'. After living in various parts of the Middle East, the Israelites settled in Canaan and formed the nation of Israel.

Philistines The Philistines were an ancient 'sea people', who sailed down the Mediterranean coast probably from what is now northern Turkey. They settled along the coast of Canaan around 1200 BC, shortly after the arrival of the Israelites, and became their major rival for power in the region. The area they occupied became known as Palestine.

Prophet In the Bible, a prophet is someone who has a special relationship with God. God spoke directly to the prophets and they passed His messages and commands to other people.

Sacrifice A sacrifice is a gift or offering made to God to worship or give thanks to Him. The sacrifice may be food or money, or it can be an animal such as a goat, which is killed. Animal sacrifice used to be part of some Jewish ceremonies. Today, people usually use the word sacrifice to describe giving up something important to them for someone else's sake.

Spirit Spirit can mean several things. The spirit of God is the essence of His power and His goodness. A spirit can also be a sort of ghost or life force that has no body, such as the evil spirit that troubled Saul.

What do you think?

These are some questions about *David and Goliath* to ask yourself and to talk about with other people.

What did God mean when He told Samuel not to judge Eliab by his appearance?

How do you think David felt when Samuel chose to anoint him and not one of his older brothers?

Why do you think David's music soothed Saul?

How would you have felt if you had heard Goliath's challenge?

Why do you think Eliab told David off? Was he right to do so?

What might have happened if David had worn Saul's armour?

Do you think Saul was pleased that David beat Goliath?

How and why is David's faith in God important in this story?

31